18 WAYS TO BECOME A MORE INTERESTING PERSON

Tom Hope

You've gotta dance like there's nobody watching, Love like you'll never be hurt, sing like there's nobody listening, and live like it's heaven on earth.

— William W. Purkey

What makes a person interesting?

Very simple answer: that person who calls attention to his culture, way of thinking, way of acting and for his pleasant personality. You don't have to be a billionaire, the CEO of Google or a pop singer for the world to admire you. Maybe you just need to change the way you live and interact with people. Look at any interesting person in your social circle and you'll notice he is:

1 – Adventurer – he likes to camp, hike, travel to different places; 2 – Generous – he does not refuse to share what he hás; looks more at others than at himself; 3 – Optimistic – he always sees the positive side, he is always happy and happy with life;

4 – Peculiar – he doesn't hide his weird side; 5 – Helpful – if you need help, he will always be there to support you and listen to you; 6 – Humble – the person who is not ashamed to wash a toilet; 7 – Resilient – if he falls seven times, eight times he will get up; 8 – Authentic – he says what he thinks; 9 – Courageous – he is not afraid of life's challenges; 10 – Self-confident – he is not afraid to be who he is and to do what he wants and when he wants.

Nobody is born interesting. This is not a gift of nature. To be an interesting person, just follow the advice presented here.

1 – Learn new skills

What can you do? Have you ever asked yourself? Let's start with the simple: do you know how to unclog a sink? That's right. It's not about composing a symphony or writing a book like "War and Peace", it's about doing simple but useful things.

Think of the following situation: you are at a barbecue. Suddenly, someone chokes on the meat. Nobody knows what to do to help that person. If you know the Heimlich maneuver, you will be the most interesting person at the barbecue. That's the idea: learn simple but useful things.

Here's a list of things you can learn: Changing a car tire; Fry an egg (yes, there are adults who don't know this, maybe even you); Basic first aid procedures; Start a fire without matches or a lighter; Make a drink, like Cosmopolitan, Cuba Libre or Margarita; Light your charcoal with a paper towel and cooking oil; Jump start a car; Use compass; Tie a tie; Change shower head.

2 – Be a dancer

At a party, the most interesting people aren't the ones leaning against the wall with a glass in their hand. Someone who can dance is an interesting person, don't you agree?

You meet a man and think "this guy is not special". Then the music starts and he asks a woman to dance. When the song ends, you see this man differently. Do you really want to surprise others? Be a good dancer. Unfortunately, you won't become a wonderful dancer by watching videos on the internet. First, because you need a partner; second, even if you have someone to practice with, this person must know how to dance. Join a dance class. It is worth it.

3 – Practice a sport

A sedentary lifestyle doesn't make anyone interesting. Only companies that run ads on TV are interested in sedentary people. After all, they are the ones who spend most of their time on the living room sofa. But an athletic person who practices sports, who has health and energy, this one really draws attention. Everyone finds someone who is good at some sport interesting, whether it's table tennis, boxing, cycling or basketball.

There are a lot of sports you can play. An easy and cheap sport, undoubtedly, is walking. You can say "but walking is not a sport". We're not talking about that walk you take to the bakery or the corner market. We're talking about putting on walking shoes, shorts and a t-shirt, grab a bottle of water and go for a walk. You need to walk until you sweat.

You don't have to be a Tom Brady in football or a Michael Jordan in basketball to get attention and be special. You just need to be good. "But how can I be good at a sport?" Lots of training.

The trick is to find a sport that you really enjoy, so training won't be boring, on the contrary, it will be something pleasurable and fun. Before starting any sport, see a doctor and have a basic check-up.

4 – Don't be ashamed of your oddities

There is no reason to be ashamed of your "weirdnesses", because they are what make you different from others. Most young people like pop and rap music. Wouldn't it be a little weird for a 16-year-old boy to say he likes Beethoven?

Imagine being embarrassed to tell your friends that instead of watching the Lady Gaga concert, you'd rather watch a Symphony Orchestra performance. Don't be ashamed of your preferences, your tastes, and your personal choices. If you like to wear socks with flip-flops, go ahead, if someone finds it weird, what does it matter to you?

We all have our oddities. It's part of life. Interesting people don't hide it. We are not in the army to dress, talk, and act alike. Admit you like to eat fried bananas for lunch or that you, even though you're a macho, like to wear nail polish.

5 – Learn another language

It's surprising when you show you can speak another language. If they then find out that you can watch a German movie without subtitles and dubbing, they will think you came from Mars. We will not deceive you here and say that learning German is easy. It's not easy at all. If you really want to learn German, or any other language, like Spanish, French or Portuguese, get ready for a long journey of studies and persistence.

On Google Play you will find hundreds of apps that teach other languages. And most of these apps are free. In this learning through cell phones, success will depend on your study routine and your commitment.

Of course, you also have the option of enrolling in a language school and receiving face-to-face lessons. The important thing is to take the first step. Learning another language will not only make you an interesting person, it will also enrich your work resume.

6 – Ask good questions

At a party or meeting with company colleagues, don't talk about yourself. If you really want to be an interesting person, don't go around bragging.

Instead, when talking to someone, ask good questions. Good questions are sensible questions. Be careful not to pry or ask uncomfortable questions.

If you know Michael plays an instrument, ask him when he got into music, where did he learn to play, what are his favorite genres. Listen to the answers carefully. Show interest. It might not be a big deal for you to play the harmonica, but for Michael, it's something special.

Another example of a good question is simply asking what you don't know instead of pretending you know everything. Say:

"Teach me how to do?" or "Can I learn from you?"

7 – Listen and be empathetic

If you want people to be interested in you, then show interest in them too. Let's take the example of Facebook. You complain no one likes your Facebook posts when, in fact, you don't like any other posts either.

Spend two months liking, sharing, and commenting on your friends' Facebook posts. Read what they are saying and comment. Show genuine interest in your friends' thoughts.

Don't be alarmed if the number of likes on your posts increases. This also works in real life. The more you care about the lives of others, the more others will be interested in you. It's a foolproof equation.

Listen carefully and understand Mary's point of view. Understand her motivations. Understand her feelings. How do you feel when you go to talk to John and he pays more attention to his cell phone than to you? Consider this the next time someone comes to talk to you.

8 – Get together with different people

One reason you don't feel like an "interesting person" is that your usual friends don't give you the right amount of appreciation.

Let's go further, maybe not even your family values you. It's common. Siblings disdain the youngest that plays the guitar. The father and mother who don't care about their son's taste for the Performing Arts. Try to interact with people who share the same interests as you. Challenge yourself to look for a new "gang". This effort is rewarding. Don't be shy about approaching and offering friendship. Don't be afraid to ask if you can "join" the group. Besides meeting new people, you will live amazing experiences.

9 – Have a good mood

It's not always easy to see the "good side" of life, is it? Sometimes the bar is too heavy. Sometimes it's hard to smile. But if you can, try to laugh, even in difficult situations. Exercise your optimism, look at the glass half full, say to yourself: "tomorrow will be another day".

Don't stress over little things. Don't ruin your day because of traffic.

Don't stop smiling because you didn't get what you wanted. There will be new opportunities.

Look at your friends and acquaintances: don't be surprised if the person you like the most is the "peace and love" type, the one who says "don't worry, it's fine". Someone who is a jokester and doesn't take life so seriously.

When you get up in the morning, say to yourself: "today I promisse no one will can break my good mood".

10 – Cheer up your environment

Be a cheerful and high-spirited person. Be unpredictable, bold. Don't be frowning, silent, looking down. Keep your head up, a smile on your face, your eyes wide open. When speaking, speak in a lively way. Be the opposite of monotonous.

Be that guy who invites his friends to happy hour, to a barbecue. Be the woman who turns up the radio volume when an exciting song plays. Try to cheer up your work environment, make jokes to make life lighter.

11 – Do not complain

Is there anything more boring than a person who just complains and complains and complains? Complains that the sun is too hot. Complains that it's raining. That it's cold. The prices are high. That the salary is low. That no one appreciates her. That the husband is lazy. That the wife doesn't clean the house properly.

Stop bothering others because gas is expensive, the price of steak has gone up, traffic is stopped, my son is this, my wife is that, I don't like this, blah, blah, blah...

Is it worth complaining? If you complained that gas was expensive and the next day the price dropped, then we would ask you to keep complaining. Does the price of gas go down every time you complain? Does the sun come up when you complain about the rain? Is it cold when you complain that the day feels like an oven?

Interesting people don't complain. Interesting people make changes. They change their lifestyle. They change the places they go. They move house. Change jobs. Change friends.

If the price of meat is high, Mary doesn't complain to the neighbor. She prioritizes chicken, eggs and vegetables. If the price of gas is high, Frank doesn't complain at the dentist's front desk. He buys a bike to work. If you think your salary is low, don't complain to the boss or colleagues at the company. Instead, take courses, seminars, improve your resume, and look for a better job. Instead of complaining, change!

12 – Say what you think and feel

"Follow the crowd." Who doesn't know this person? He is the one who agrees with everyone, who lets himself be convinced by the first argument presented. Perhaps it is easier for lightning to strike twice in the same place than for him to raise his hand to disagree with the group.

We can even say that he is the person who makes no difference in his environment. This guy can be anything but interesting. So, if you really want to be worthy of attention, defend your opinions. Say out loud "I don't like that", "I prefer another alternative", "I don't agree with that", "I think differently", and so on.

Don't get that ridiculous fear of "not being accepted" by the group. If your friends don't respect your opinions and tastes, it means they don't respect you. And if your friends don't respect you, what friends are they?

You respect yourself when you stand up for your opinions, expose your thoughts, say how you feel. And those who respect themselves impose respect.

13 – Go Travel

Do you have money left over at the end of the year? Go travel. Forget Disney. Go to a different place. Go to another country. Cross the Atlantic if your budget allows. "Oh, but I can't speak French, Italian, German..." No problem. What are tour guides for? Buy a travel package and go without fear. Try the local cuisine. Visit museums. Visit historic sites. Learn about their history. Try to absolve as much of the culture as you can.

Unable to travel abroad? Alright, get to know more about the US. And to make things more "interesting", choose destinations that almost no one knows about. Four out of five friends can say they've been to New York, Los Angeles or Miami, but only you can say you've visited

Willamette National Forest - Oregon, or Devil's Tower - Wyoming.

Take many pictures. Take notes. Post these photos on your social media. When you get back, print the photos and spread them around your house.

14 – Read

If you have the money and the willingness to travel, great. But if not, read! Reading is also a journey. And the internet is there to be your means of transport.

Fill your head with knowledge. In a few clicks on Google, you can find out why the Roman Empire ended; who was Saladin; when and where the Crusades took place. You can access photos and maps of historical events. When we talk about reading, we also talk about literature. Besides reading about history, you had to read books of short stories, novels, and science fiction. Literary baggage is healthy for your brain. Try reading Moby-Dick by Herman Melville. Read Robert Frost's poems, Flannery O'Connor's short stories.

15 – Spend time with interesting people

You are influenced by the surrounding people. If you spend a lot of time with a person who talks screaming and swears at every sentence, you will unconsciously start saying "go to hell" or "fu** you" more often. If you spend more time with nice, smart, polite and kind people, guess what happens?

Discover interesting people and join them. And where to find these people? For example, we previously talked about getting into a language school. Your language classmates will be interesting people with whom you can make friends. We also talk about reading. Imagine how cool you are to be part of a book club in your city? Imagine talking to people who read the same book as you?

As you follow the advice presented here, you will automatically come into contact with other interesting people who are also on this beautiful journey in searching for happier, healthier, and more cultured life.

16 – Go deep in your interests

Think of someone interesting. Perhaps what makes this person so special in your eyes is that he has a grand passion in life. There are people who are passionate about helping in nursing homes, hospitals and churches.

Imagine you meet someone who is passionate about spending their Saturday, their day off, at the nursing home... Spending the day talking to the elderly, helping them to walk, helping them to eat... That person wouldn't be interesting?

Now think about your friend who is a music freak. Leisure for him is spending the day studying musical scores.

Find something that really gives you pleasure and motivation. Let's take a simple example. Imagine a boy who is a rock fan. He doesn't know how to play any instrument; he understands nothing about rhythm and his voice is out of tune. One day he wakes up and says "I want to delve into rock history". So he runs to the internet and starts researching. He wants to know who was the first rock band, who invented rock, when it spread, who are the biggest icons, what are the subgenres of rock. And he doesn't just want to read, he wants to listen, so he buys CDs, DVDs, downloads songs and videos from each band, he does analysis; he gives notes; he goes to shows, anyway... The guy goes deep into his passion for rock. And this entire process doesn't happen in weeks or months. This passion he will carry for years. Every day he will want to learn more about rock.

You got it? Swap rock for any other genre. Swap for a specific band or singer. Swap even for a hobby. You say "I like to take things apart and see how they work". Excellent. Go deep. Buy tools, set up a small workshop. Join electronic courses. Choose a passion and go deep, really deep.

17 – Be different

Another effective way to be interesting is to "be different". Don't feel obligated to do what everyone else does. Don't get caught up in everyday fads.

If it's fashionable to be "flaunting", with people wearing designer clothes and expensive sneakers, carrying gold necklaces and bracelets, do the opposite, wear simple clothes. Don't be a walking jewelry display. If it's fashionable to wear thick-rimmed, tortoiseshell glasses, go for thin-rimmed glasses. There are a lot of little things in our daily lives we can do differently. It could even be the way you tie your shoelace. The way you hold your hair. You shave. It could even be the way to greet. Instead of saying the simple "Hello, how are you doing?" say, "Good to see you. How is your force?"

18 – Share your experiences

If someone asks you "how was your weekend?" don't answer with a simple "it was nice." Say "gosh, I read a fantastic book that had me hooked from beginning to end". "I watched a thriller movie that made my head spin." "I visited an Italian restaurant, and I had the best pasta of my life".

Share your life, your experiences. Say what you experienced, what you did, and what you saw. It doesn't matter if it was bad or good. You can also share this experience "I went to that city and I can only say one thing: what a damn place, there is nothing special there."

"The show of that band was a disappointment. I expected more". "The ending screwed up the whole movie". "I swear I'll never go to that restaurant again. Cold, tasteless food."

Be careful not to boast. You don't have to get on a pedestal to say you've done cool things, implying that you're an important and special person for your experiences. The trick here is for you to share your experiences and encourage others to live those experiences as well. Say:

"I had my fears about Japanese food, but after eating sushi, I'm in love. Have you ever tried Japanese food? No? Why don't you come with me to that restaurant, it'll be cool."

Share your experiences and invite others to be a part of those experiences.

Being interesting

You must have realized that it will not be a simple task to be an interesting person. You may have to change your lifestyle. Keep one thing in mind: others won't find you an interesting person overnight. This takes a while. It all depends on your persistence in following the advice presented here.

Don't be discouraged if, in the first few weeks, others don't look at you with more admiration, even if you follow the advice presented here. Incorporate this advice into your habits. And for that to happen, you must practice every day. Gradually, you will notice changes in your style and personality. Then, after months, you yourself will realize that you are someone interesting and worthy of attention.

18 WAYS TO BECOME A MORE INTERESTING PERSON

TOM HOPE

ALL RIGHTS RESERVED